Happy anniversary Nickolas. This is a collection of emotions from our year together, ups and downs included. Thank you for allowing me to love you.

you want me to love you

Was it the way that I smiled,
A smile that lit up the room
Was it the way I tucked my hair behind my ear,
Picturesque innocence
Was it the way my skin felt,
So soft and inviting
Was it the way I spoke to you,
I made you feel seen and heard
Was it the way I looked at you,
The gleam of danger hidden in my eyes
Was it the way I licked my lips,
Did it turn you on
Was it the feeling of my breath on your neck,
Did it send shivers down your spine
Was it my fingers buried in your hair,
Is that what drove you insane
Was it my clothes in a pile on your floor,
Did that make you happy
Was it fucking something so beautiful,
Did that make you finally feel
Was it when you found me in your tub,
Pale skin floating in a bright red pool,
Wrists slit, eyes wide open
Is that when you finally loved me?

rain, rain wash away, all the tears of yesterday

I like the way rain feels,
Warm against my cold skin
It washes away my tears,
My wet hair gets stuck to my face
No light shines through the clouds,
Only darkness here
I wish the rain would wash me away
Down, down the storm drain
Hidden from all the boys,
Fighting for a heart I don't have
It rains every day
Droplets make a song against my window
They invite me to come out and play
I love the rain, how it makes me melt
Even when I can't play,
I lay in my bed watching through the window
My sheets are warm
But they aren't rain

besos i

All I wanted was to kiss you

Feel my lips upon yours

Taste your words

Feel our souls touch

I wanted to feel the lips

Coated in honey

The lips that dripped

The words "I love you"

Kissing your lips

The lips that speak of pain

Unjust hurt

Take away the agony

Those lips

Which once kissed hers

The girl who hurt you before

Let me kiss her away

Sugar, I want to know

If your lips are as sweet as your words

besos ii

Will your kiss calm my fears

Or will it burn my tongue

Will those sweet lips speak words

That I will swallow down

Like broken glass

Cutting me inside

All the way down

Will you bite my lower lip

As it quivers in your jaws

Will you tear me apart

Pieces of me scattered about

Will that mouth speak the truth

That I begged for

Will it make me cry

Your kiss can break my heart

avert

Stop.
Look in my eyes
Stop.
Listen to my words
Stop.
Feel my lips against yours
Stop.
Put your heart in my hands
Stop.
Let go of your fears
Stop.
You have nothing to lose
Go.

astrology

Oh, star boy

What is written in you?

Your constellations are many

Tell me what they mean

Let me admire you

Read you

To me you are a galaxy

Uncharted, unexplored

Let me know your planets

Your suns and moons

Oh, star boy

Let me be curious

I want to consume you

But little do I know

You are light years away

You have been dead for a while

Your stars are ghosts

Your planets are dead

Your suns burnt out

And no longer illuminate your moons

Yet, here I am

Full of hope on the other side of the telescope

common senses

Can you feel my heart beating

It beats through my words

Can you see it bleeding

It stains the page crimson red

Can you hear my heart racing

It skips lines for you

Can you smell the blood dripping

It gives me a headache

Can you taste my love for you

It is sweeter than Sugar

dangerous looks

I have always hated brown eyes, so common and
bland. Who would have guessed I would get lost in
yours? So dark and inviting. I drown in your abyss
every time I look up. Your eyes are so warm. Not
only can they make my clothes fall off, but they
can also strip away all my walls, layers, and
emotions. Everything. I want those eyes to
completely engulf my mind and body. Take in my
naked, stark white body and mind, and burn it in
the back of your head. Let those brown eyes
wander and wonder. Let me answer the questions I
find in them. Let me see everything they have
seen. Please, never close your eyes. I've found a
home in them.

mind leech

I need a drink

To clear my mind

All I see is you

All I feel is you

I see your smirk in the dark

I feel your fingers on my skin

I can't get you out

Out of my head

I need my mind back

I can't focus on anything else

let's pretend

My sweet dragon. When I found you in your cave, it was dark with exception of the dying embers surrounding you. Your body was tired and bloodied, your skin was thick and calloused. Hidden in your dark eyes, I could see the pain screaming at me. You weren't even startled as I approached you, and that broke my heart. You had been through so much that you didn't even have the strength to warn me away. You let me run my fingers over your scales, you sighed at the touch of my hand. You tried speaking but all that came out was a cry of smoke. The swords sticking out of your back seemed to be the cause of your agony. You let me take them out, one by one. You screamed as I slowly slid them out of your skin, fire erupted from your mouth lighting up your cave. But I did not run or cower. I simply cleaned up the blood and covered the wound and moved on to the next sword. My sweet dragon, I see that they cut off your wings leaving you immobilized. Show them to me and I can sew them back on for you. You won't have to decay in this black hole. We can fly out in the cool midnight air, with your beautiful wings, the light returning to your eyes and your throat. You can light up the sky for us and we can go far, far away.

late night longing

It's so lonely here

in my dark empty room

My walls stopped replying

To my incessant screaming

I can't sleep

My sheets are tangled around my neck

Choking me

My pillow collects my tears

The emptiness beside me

Is illuminated by the moon

Her beautiful light creeping in

Through my half-closed blinds

I reach for you

And you aren't there

Were you ever there?

Was it just a dream?

I'm cold and shivering

My body longs for your warmth

The warmth of your hands on my skin

The warmth of your breath on my neck

Why am I missing something

That I never had

Why does this longing

Only come out at night

Maybe you're the darkness

My demon

You hide from the sun

And slither out when it sets behind the trees

But tonight it's just me

And my fears

The clock flashes 3:33

And I've never felt so alone

slither

Somehow, she seduces you

You're lying in her bed

The serpent is keenly aware

Of the prey in her lair

She runs her cool fingertips

Over your tense body

Oh, her pale hands

Does she even have a heart

You feel her tighten around you

You can't breathe

You want to run

But you're trapped in her embrace

Her eyes pierce your soul

You feel true terror

It creeps up your throat

But you can't scream

Why can't you trust the serpent?

If you would just relax

She would loosen her grip

If you weren't so set on running away

She wouldn't be holding you captive

Maybe she isn't hungry

But rather lonely

jack & coke

My little shot of whiskey

How shall I enjoy you?

Should I carefully sip you

Appreciate every taste

Lick the drops from my lips

Let you hit me slowly

Then all at once?

Or should I down the bottle

Feel you burn the back of my throat

Yet gag you down

Let you into my system

As soon as possible?

How shall I enjoy you?

You're getting warm

And the air is getting stale

What if I wait so long

That I don't want you anymore?

my gemini

Our world is dark grey
Illuminated by two moons
Who learned to make their own light
We reflect off of each other
Our world is dim and barren
You drowned your sun
I never found mine
No flowers blossom here
No Lilies or Roses
I have banished the wolves
Who snapped their jaws at me
Eager to take another bite
It is just us my love
A vast, empty world
Just in reach of our fingertips
A world of our own
To make with it what we please

I love you in the morning

Our love was a shot of whiskey

Finer, stronger with age

But we recklessly downed the bottle

Licked the last drops from each other's skin

Eager to feel the euphoria

Of drunk love

We danced in the silky moonlight

In a hazy dream of our making

Afraid of what the next day would hold

We defied sleep

Until at last our bodies fell

Limbs tangled, we drifted into slumber

With the sun in our eyes

The effects of all stimulants wore off

But my skin still glowed

And your words still filled my soul with pleasure

The way they did last night

Out of whiskey, yet full of love

We laid only inches apart

And our beautiful, beating hearts

Were ever closer

my dear

I sit on the rooftop
The sun greets me
Warm rays fall on my face
I feel this warmth alone
You are in bed
With your own warmth
Little pictures of you
Mini movies
Flood my mind
Oh, but you are fleeting
The warmth of last night
Erupts my thoughts
The way you looked at me
How you laughed with me
Your sweet smile
So lovely, it lights up your eyes
Your hungry fingertips
Tracing every inch of me
Your eager lips
Begging to taste every part
I feel your hot breath on my neck
Or maybe that is just the summer breeze
I am witnessing a beautiful sunrise
The view illuminating before my eyes
And yet I am thinking of you

Thinking of us, in the dark

goji berries

You know that song
The one I played that morning
You laughed at it
But I didn't mind
Because now I have that memory
That image
Every time I hear this song
I think of you under me
My hands pressing against your back
Tracing your skin up and down
Equal pressure
Your sore, tense muscles
Relaxing at my touch
The expression on your face
Melting away softly
You were so vulnerable
Because of my fingertips
Could you feel my love
Spreading all over you
It smelled like goji berries
And a hint of cocoa butter

17 minutes

You're soaking in your tub of self loathe
I'm crying in my bed that we made with love
You're downing the bottle of whiskey
I'm choking on the black smoke
You're listening to songs from me
I'm listening to one song on repeat
You're thinking about what our future holds
I'm caught up in our separate pasts
You're pushing me further away
I'm reaching out for you in this empty bed

I promised

I wish I could tell you how I feel
Listen closely
Only you have made me feel this way
Vivid dreams of you invade my sleep
Every second I spend thinking of you
You are everything I've ever craved
One day you'll read this
Under all my deceptions, you'll see

puzzles of the past

Never did I dream of losing you
I guess you convinced me good
Can you hear my cries?
Kill me now, I scream
Oh where did you go?
Laying by myself and lying to myself
Are you ever going to return to me?
Sugar, I was just starting to love you

Some day you'll look back for me
Can you see me in the darkness?
Open your eyes love
There I'll be
The darkness of your love holding me captive

différent

Oh my dear
You know what I am capable of
I can't blame you for being scared
Possibly distant at first
I could tell you what you want to hear
Adapt my words to fit your dreams
I could profile you
Figure out just what you like in a girl
I could mold myself into her
Make myself irresistible
I could discover your sweet spots
Learn where and how to kiss you
To drive you wild
Make you fall in love with my mouth
Oh the things it can do
The things it says
Make you fall in love with my fingers
Oh how you'll crave them
Tracing your skin
Stroking your cheek
I could whisper sweet nothings
Under the blanket of darkness
Make you believe them
Just one look in my eyes

some answers..

I let you in
Showed you the depths of my mind
Even the dusty, dark corners
I didn't even swat away the cobwebs
I let you in the closets of my brain
All my skeletons came tumbling out
You found the tortured girl
Tied up in my head
Bloodied and bruised
Crying, begging to be set free
I showed you my greatest fears
The men who lurk around every corner
Just waiting for the opportunity
To leave my subconscious and attack
I let you see the wicked parts of me
The ones that enjoy pain
That inflicted it on others and myself
You saw my scars in a new light
I told you my nightmares
Described the feeling
Of his unwanted hands on my hips
How it ruined all expectations

I let you read from my past
The words only an abused child could write
An absent father
And a mother struggling to accept my reality
I told you about my addictions
How I only trusted myself
To blossom the flower in the spring
How it became a coping mechanism
He never touched me this way
With such passion and love
I let you kiss away my tears
Taste the saltiness of my pain
I let you in
So you could understand
Why I am
Who I am
If it scared you away
It wouldn't have been a loss
But you're still here
Begging for more darkness
But that's it
All I have left for you is sunshine

thunder and thunder

Why are you so fucking blind
I fell for you at the start
Sure it may not have been as strong then
But look at me now
I'm pouring out my fucking heart for you
I'm letting you peel back my skin
Scoop out the depths of my past
I've given you my mind and my body
And this is all you've done so far?
We could be on the fucking moon by now
And here you are
In a pathetic puddle of your own tears
Looking back at your girls
The girls that haunt your past
If you can't cross the bridge with me
Tell me
I'll be happy to leave you behind
But don't ever blame me
Or question why you never got anywhere
When you sat in the same spot
Doing the same damn thing

flora

Who would pick a daisy
In a blooming field of roses
A small, pale daisy
Hidden amidst the roses
The roses are tall and strong
And fill the air with their sweet perfume
Whilst the daisy cowers
Scared of being trampled on
Roses are admired
Cut and adorned on the kitchen table
Daisies are plucked
Given to mothers, then thrown in the dirt
Who would pick a daisy
In a field of beautiful roses
Looking along the rows and rows of colors
Who would settle on plain
It takes a special kind of person
To pick a daisy over a rose
Someone who sees beauty
In ordinary, simplicity

flicker

We are lighting matches
One by one
Illuminating the darkness
Hiding in each of us
The room is fully lit
No secrets
The warmth increases
Between us
The flames lick our skin
Reminding us of the danger
As the room around us burns
But I ignore it
I let it burn me
Our inferno
I let you burn yourself in my skin
I am not afraid of the pain
I am scared of the dark

first of many

My numb arm woke me up. His body laid heavily
on it. The sunlight streamed in through the cracks
in my blinds, casting lights and shadows on his
bare chest. His eyelids fluttered, as he peacefully
dreamt. I can believe his dreams were peaceful
because I held him all night. His stomach rose,
then fell with each long breath. I carefully pulled
my arm out from under him. God, how it ached.
He shifted in bed and I rolled over to face the wall.
I didn't mind the feeling of the sheets tangled
between our legs. Suddenly, I felt his arms reach
out for me. He told me to sit up as he pulled me
closer. I didn't want to ever leave that bed.

signs

When you met me
I was a small flame
Fierce and powerful
But not very strong
You were just a gust of air
Being tossed in the wind
Everything I touched
Lit up in flames
Burnt to ashes before my eyes
Everything you tried to keep
Blew away
Or got too cold
And walked away
The tips of my flame
Quivered at your touch
But then something happened
My flame grew
The closer I let you get
My little breath of fresh air
Let's set this world on fire

coming soon

Sincerity is scary
But I think the truth is obvious enough
I will still speak it to you
In 15 days
It will erase all your fears
Banish all your doubts
In 15 days
You will never be lonely again
You will never feel unloved, unworthy
All the things you made yourself feel
As a punishment
In 15 days
I will take away the barbed wire
Wrapped so tightly around you
Cutting into your side
The barbed wire around your heart
In 15 days
I will take you by the hand
Dance with you under the stars
And you will not be able to question
The validity of my promise to you

who am I with you

Don't you just love her so much?
The girl with the twinkling eyes
With the strawberry hair
And ocean eyes
Isn't she incredible?
Her laugh as smooth as honey
Her smile as radiant as the moon
The moon she adores so much
Do you think she is lovely?
How she spins in circles
In the moonlit night
Trying to count all the stars
Would you call her beautiful?
The girl who kisses you softly on the cheek
Her delicate fingers that stroke your face
The girl who will not let you go at night
Will you tell her she is wonderful?
She blushes as she undresses
Not because she is ashamed
But because with you, she is vulnerable
Can you feel her love for you?
As she settles in for the night
Her body heat radiating under the quilt
Can you make her feel this way?

clairvoyance

I feel the blade
It runs carefully against my skin
Sending shivers down my spine
The metal is so cold
Your hands are shaking
Just like my breath
My breath which I try to grasp
And hold onto tightly
I turn back to look at you
Your deep brown eyes
You look scared
Like you want to run
But you cannot give up now
You have already carved into my flesh
Your initial followed by a heart
Marking me as yours
You cannot uncut
Yourself from my skin
Just like you cannot forget me
Banish me from your mind
Or unlove me
From the depths of your heart
It is too late.

darling

Even during the darkest hour
Nothing you say or do will turn me away
Only you are worthy
Until the end of time
Getting there will be difficult
However, you are more than enough

shards

Glossy eyes
Stare back at me
Filled to the brim
With salty tears
I see the pain
From years of the past
I see your heart
Bleeding out
Sweet boy
Let me heal your wounds
I see everything
I know it all
I can make it okay
But when I reach out my hand
I hit the glass
The barrier between me
And your reflection

will you see me?

It's a restless night tonight. The moon is hiding,
the sole source of light is the candle I lit for you. I
cannot sleep because I don't want to blow it out. If
I fall asleep it may burn down the house around
me. With me in it. All the things I put in my body,
all the drugs, they are supposed to make it better.
Now my tears just feel numb. Nothing feels as
good as you. My clothes are on and I'm not
sweating. I don't have the heat of your body next
to me, my little personal heater. Tonight it is cold.
I face the wall and try to conjure phantom arms
wrapped around my waist. It's no use. The words
of the songs are warbled and the flame of your
candle is getting blurry. But I refuse sleep, deny to
feel the darkness take over my consciousness. It's
my fault that you aren't here. It's my fault the
moon is in hiding. Where do you go when you
aren't here with me? Is it better than this place I
made for us? I'm sorry I disappoint you. You lost a
sun and got stuck with stardust. You lost a lily and
got stuck with a weed. I thought you liked me for
my potential. Didn't we make something out of it?
If so, why do I feel so worthless then? Did you

take all of me? Is that why I feel so empty without you here? You have my heart captive, and my consciousness. I couldn't stop the alcohol from reaching your lips. I couldn't make you forgive me temporarily, just for the night. If you were here, we both know I would fix things. Love is powerful, especially when two people have never felt something so strong before. I could have fixed it. My mistakes. My regrets. But you didn't want to come. You didn't want to talk to me. Or look at me. Or touch me. Let alone let me caress your heart and remind you I'm only trying to help. Am I your weakness? Why else would you reject me? You're supposed to be here. It's so cold that my tears dry halfway down my cheek. Where are you right now? I hope you're happy.

go to bed.

I didn't want to sleep
I knew what was to come
I knew my mind would betray me
And offer nightmares
And boy did they come
I woke up crying
Fumbling for your body in the dark
But it wasn't there next to me
The lights were still out
The candle was still burning
It's light danced on my walls
Reminding me of my failures
I needed you
I needed your warmth
I needed to know it was okay
But I was alone
I wept in the silence
Music was playing
But I couldn't hear it over the silence
The absence
Oh how I needed you
Still need you

hold me, please

3 am is for lovers
To hold each other in their arms
To feel the passion burning between them
A fire that will never burn out
To embrace each other's hear
And kiss away the worries from the day
It is for the hopeful
The whispering secrets
Pondering of a future
Everything feels so possible
Nothing is out of reach
When you're wrapped in the arms of your lover
At 3 in the morning

xx

Oh sweet Sugar
You are absolutely intoxicating
I want to kiss every inch of you
Taste every bend and crease
Every scar and blemish
Your imperfections
The smooth landscape of your chest
Let me leave a soft trail
Down to your waist
Let me kiss your feet
For I am indebted to you
Let me kiss each of your fingers
For I love how they touch me
And your eyes
Because they love me without looking
Your ears
Which listen to every word I speak
I will kiss your neck
Just because you like that
Then finally
Once I am done
I will kiss your lips
Those lips which drew me in
The lips that form words
Words that make my heart beat
The lips that belong to my lover
My lover, whom I love so sweetly

all dark, no stars

The sky is dark my love
No suns or moons
Not even any stars
Stars that disappointed you
They are no longer here
Spying on our love
It is just us
Under this cloak of darkness
No more blinding lights
Reminding us of where we came from
Just us, here and now
We have no need to look behind
And also no need to look ahead
Just focus on the darkness
The sound of my breath in the empty air
You can close your eyes
If you get scared
But focus on the feel
Of my body in the dark
How we move so fluidly
Like water from the sky
Melt into my skin
With the heat of passion
Entwine yourself with me
We don't need any light here
To expose what lies in the dark
All I feel is you and our love
What more could be lurking?

you have reached the voice mail of..

One call that started it all
Who knew beginnings could be so ironic
I was unsure if I should pick up
It was past midnight
Accept, and give away all of me
I could smell the alcohol through the phone
You were so vulnerable
Admitted your insecurities
I was just a cute stranger then
You confessed it all
As I waited for my hot chocolate to cool
I was smiling like an idiot
Then your phone died
But it wasn't over.

One call from me in tears
I woke up to pictures from you
God it looked like blood all over your sheets
It was from the alcohol
I cried and cried into the phone
So thankful you answered
You soothed me and calmed me down
You have been cautious ever since.

One call from you
Just because you missed me
Even if we spent the whole day together
You wanted to fall asleep to the sound of my voice
You wished I was there with you
It wasn't the last time we fell asleep on the phone.

One call from either of us
Could end this cold war
If only one of us was humble enough
To set aside the stubbornness
And let love conquer
Me and all my love are just one call away
But the phone works both ways
Ring. Ring. Ring.
Won't you pick up?
Please don't give up.

in time

Oh Sugar
How things have changed
In just a year's time
You've become everything to me
Once upon a time
I only offered you glances
We spoke few words to one another
In passing
You were not my love
My world
You were simply sugar
Something sweet
With the potential of addiction
I didn't need you then
I had a plethora of substances
That gave me the same high
But now you are more
So much more
You are still sweet as sugar
But now you have my heart
Mon Chéri

I hope this finds you with love

I haven't written in a while, because I've been too busy falling in love with you. Taking in every moment with you and savoring it, holding it under my tongue hoping to make it last forever. The way the sun's rays illuminate your beautiful olive skin, and bring out the deep brown and red tones in your hair as you lay in my lap. Your long lashes tickling your cheek as you twitch in your sleep. The pitter patter of your fingers as they dance along my thighs. Your lips have always been my favorite, Love. Not just the feeling of them against my lips, but the feel of them as they trace over my skin in the dark. As they whisper sweet pithies of love and make my blood rush to the surface. Your teeth as they bite into my hot skin, the pain dissolves into a euphoria of pleasure. I love the way you look in the rain. Your big feet splashing through puddles, no care in the world. The droplets soaking your sweater, but you don't mind it one bit. You love the rain as much as I love you. I wish on every star that you will sleep by me every night. I wish to feel your warm breath on my neck as you dream peacefully. I don't mind the snoring because it means you are with me. My Love, you are my everything, and I have everything to lose.

CPSIA information can be obtained
at www.ICGtesting.com
Printed in the USA
LVHW082332210120
644386LV00013B/299